Pencil in the Air

BY

Samuel Hoffenstein

PENCIL IN THE AIR
POEMS IN PRAISE OF PRACTICALLY NOTHING
YEAR IN, YOU'RE OUT

Samuel Hoffenstein

PENCIL IN THE AIR

MCMXLVII

Doubleday & Company, Inc.

GARDEN CITY, NEW YORK

TO

ELIZABETH

A few of these verses
have appeared
in The New Yorker,
the New York Herald Tribune,
and Harper's Magazine.

Table of Contents

[9]

[10]

Proem

PROEM

Wherever I go,
I go too,
And spoil everything.

Children's Album

I

History

Besides the Lord's mysterious love,
History is a record of
The long attempt
Of Church and State
To exterminate,
Eradicate,
Extinguish and obliterate,
Expunge, annul, annihilate,
Demolish, quell and abrogate,
Dismantle, ruin and efface,
Squelch and scuttle without trace
The human race
By war and fire and rope and ax,
Wheel and water, dungeon, tax,
Hunger, terror, torment, wrong,
Despair and serfdom, thirst and thong.

To which, so runs the document,
The victim gave complete assent,
And thought
And sought
And wrought
And fought
Fiercely to co-operate
And handsomely participate!

Well, since they strive that this befall,
I wish success to one and all,
And know, when Church and State alone
Stand naked stone to naked stone,
The beasts and birds and crawling things
Will leave the proper offerings.

II

Budget

The gonad is designed to mate us,
And thereby, obviously, create us,
Whereas the mute, minute bacillus
Is admirably made to kill us:
A balanced budget in this case
Would greatly benefit the race.

III

Experience

The weirdest ills are put to rout
By having teeth and tonsils out,
But if, with teeth and tonsils banished,
The ills referred to have not vanished,
It is generally understood
The operation did no good.

IV

Birds

An ostrich on his native sand
Is worth a couple in the hand;
The same is applicable to
The minatory marabou,
Although the proverb may insist
A bird is worth more in the fist.

V

The Saddle

Capital, Labor, Rich or Poor,
Rightist, Leftist, East or West,
Death and taxes and this are sure—
Who sits in the saddle rides herd on the rest.

Cross or Crescent, Dragon or Sickle,
Brawn or Brains or Stricken or Blest—
The Hand that turns the wheel is fickle:
Who sits in the saddle rides herd on the rest.

Sadist or Saviour, Layman, Priest,
The Devil-damned or the God-possessed—
The feast of Power is a heady feast:
Who sits in the saddle rides herd on the rest.

The few or the many, the Right or Wrong,
The Justice-driven, the Hate-confessed—
The song of Power is a siren song:
Who sits in the saddle rides herd on the rest.

Fellow creature and desperate foe,
Death is a terror, so live we must,
But this is a truth we hide and know—
We sit in the saddle or lie in the dust.

VI

A Little (Not Much) about the Ladies

Women have three years to hope in;
The fourth, they leap into the open,
And hence, by masculine acclaim,
Leap year gets its name and fame,
Although, with subtle skill in mating,
They pull some fast ones, too, while waiting.

VII

Fifth Commandment

Love your parents, not as such,
But since like you, forlorn,
They too began this life in dutch,
Not asking to be born.

[22]

The Oceans

The oceans, like necrophilists,
Paw dead shores and breed dead mists;
The mineral eyes of darkness stare
As blind as bats on barren air—
Thus do the seas and stars equip
The studious mind for statesmanship.

IX

Cradle Song

Fear not the atom in fission;
The cradle will outwit the hearse;
Man on this earth has a mission—
To survive and go on getting worse.

X

Geopolitics

Birds live in air and fish in water,
Somebody's son in somebody's daughter,
The tasseled corn in corn fritters,
The caterpillar on front-porch sitters,
Americans, in ice-cold cokes,
The farmer's daughter in watchfob jokes,

Good intentions in obvious louses,
Tillamook deaths in doomèd mouses,
Tergiversations, equivocations,
In the relations between nations,
Anfractuosities in harried
Loving couples legally married,
Termites in rented, high-priced homes,
Nonsense and blight in holy domes,
Massed men and women in headline hordes,
Statesmen in hand-sprayed vocal chords,
Pigs in clover and clover in pigs,
Adult folk in bent twigs,
Illusions, when the blossoms fall,
In jury-duty and alcohol,
The sound scratch in the sound itch,
And sainthood in the stony niche.

Most of us live, with troubled breath,
In hope of dying a painless death.

XI

From the Chinese

No taxee—no lendee—
No gottee—no spendee.

XII

Effect of Humans on Animals, on the Universe and on the Author

I. ON ANIMALS

The antics of the human race
Bespectacle the house-fly's face,
Who peers bemused at me and you
And dives bewildered into glue;
The hare essays in vague unease
Continuous carnalities,
And nibbles, while his ear observes,
Lettuce for his jumpy nerves;
The termite, cowering with the mouse,
Runs amok, brings down the house;
The headlines scampering through his head,
The goat becomes more capriped,
Disdains the tin can on his table
Because he dreads the printed label;
The horse instinctively inveighs
Against you with emphatic neighs;
The zany lion in the zoo
Attempts a roar, achieves a moo;
Fish, large and small, in fronded seas,
Stare at your Bikinanities,
Your spin-the-top uncertainties
At silly water weirdly hurled,
And think the mushroom is the world;
Even the dog, whom Nature meant
To be at ease and reticent,
Tries his confusion to dispel
With baffled barks of doggerel,
And, Nightmare's neurasthenic own,
Gnaws for the answer at a bone.

Two billion people, black and white,
Bi-sexual, male, and parasite,
Dismay the earth, astound the sea,
Bewilder Death and chisel me!

XIII

Statesman

Sired by Narcissus, Demos-dam'd, he stands
And primps for history before the herd,
The rabbit of salvation in his hands
Extracted from the empty, silken word,

Or, like the pigeons in the pepper trees,
Perched on his high confusions, drearily
Regurgitating rancid elegies,
Drops nostrums on the demagogracy.

Madrigal Macabre

MADRIGAL MACABRE

Some want a vault, some want a grave,
Bold sailors the sepulchral wave;
To some cold lives it has hotly mattered
That they be burned and their ashes scattered;
Some souls bemused with fear of haunts
Want to be buried beside their aunts;
Most urban jokers, treys and deuces
Want to be laid under hometown spruces;
Pharaohs stanch and Pharaohs fickle
Agreed upon a permanent pickle,
Surrounded by such lesser dills
As needful to their royal wills;
Some want a headstone, some a slab,
Some flowers, some rice—as good, but drab;
Some want a funeral de luxe,
Some specify but dogs and cooks;
Some want violent lamentation,
Some a muted murmuration;
Some wills grow jolly and complete
With wakes and hot, baked funeral meat,
With women keening and men drinking
And the corpse, as it imagines, winking;
Some want show and some deceases
Want neither choir nor Rest-in-Peaces;
Some, dying, feel their own tears flow
At thought of a pal saying, "Good old Joe!";

Some will not close a final eye
Until assured their graves are dry;
Some who know gardens and manure
Are partial to damp sepulture;
Some would like the works entire,
Burial, mausoleum, pyre,
The gloved cortege, the plumèd horse,
The lodges out in splendid force—
But I, who have but thinly thrived,
Should much prefer to be revived.

Desert Song

DESERT SONG

After the trouble and the tears,
After the wraths and the wraiths depart,
Peace, nurtured by the lonely years,
Blooms like a cactus in the heart

And pierces all—what dreams, what truth,
What hopes and joys yet dare to keep
The vigil of remembered youth,
Until they gently bleed to sleep.

The Grail

THE GRAIL

Together we have learned, where nettles grow;
Where not the vanished, but the living sup,
What Galahad, enchanted, did not know:
The Grail is in the seeking, not the Cup.

＊

Autobiography with Adjuration
or
Emergency Measure
or
O Congress Give the Children Beer

AUTOBIOGRAPHY WITH ADJURATION
or
EMERGENCY MEASURE
or
O CONGRESS, GIVE THE CHILDREN BEER

Now sinks the sun (and so do I—
And what does not?) and in the sky
The stars like little lambs appear
And baa to the poetic ear,
While I, reduced by sundry woes
To tweedy verse and tattered prose,
Survey, like the insensate sod,
The grand, nocturnal style of God,
As deaf, as blind, when Beauty calls,
As if I were Niagara Falls.

So what? So then, I stand and stare
Upon the buildings and the air
And wonder, in the global gloom,
Why men create, then damn their doom;
Why simple meanings of the world,
Like flags of fallen armies furled,
Lie on the shelves of little minds
While Chaos her own flag unwinds;
Why failing faiths and feet should tread
The huge synopsis of the dead;

[41]

Why they who hew or heal or pull
Be empty when the earth is full;
Why bloodiest war could not make taut
The texture of the common thought;
Until at last I take to bed
The clamant sparrows in my head
And count, amid the jeers of Sleep,
What's left to count? the tax on sheep,
A goat or two, confined in banks,
For transfer to the income blanks.

So then? (Oh, let a fellow rhyme
Some small diversion out of Time!)
So then—O bardlings, go and bait your
Need of joy with dreams of Nature—
With honey-hauling, solvent bees;
With reeds and roses, rain and trees
And birds who stir their leaves with song,
As cuckoo as the day is long,
Or those who owl throughout the night
Their avian dirges of delight;
With sun and shade and stream and lake
And wood—and give yourselves a brake!
But not for me, when times appal,
The whippoorwill and waterfall,
Cathartic palm or unguent pine—
Another subterfuge is mine
When the volcanic days require
A quick hegira from the fire,
And Thought, in undershirt and pants,
Must flee the Furies and Finance—
For then, in wistful dream, I fly
Hot-foot before the doleful I
And find (O beatific boon!)
A refuge in the old Saloon!

O happy shelter, hallow'd cove,
The heart's deflated treasure-trove,
The gentle Growler's mirror'd cave,
Home of the hopped and malted brave,
Not of the rapture and the rest
You poured into the adult breast
I mumble on my cracked bassoon,
But of my childhood joys, Saloon,
When as a tot I tottered in
And with an upward-pointing chin,
As needle to the northern star,
Was magnetized unto the bar!
There, like a mariner inspired,
By Davil Sea to frenzy fired,
I stood upon the rail, surveyed
The billowing schooner unafraid,
Disdained the alien corn, and home
Plunged into the siren foam.
O plushy foam, O hurricane blow,
O splash upon the floor below
Around the inviolate spittoon;
O squadron gait, O triple moon
Revealed above the swinging door
(O triple crescent, sometimes four),
O nubile hiccup, meek and mild,
Confessing the transported child,
That like a frightened mouse would start
And melt to love the hardest heart;
O infant playmates gathered round
A foot above the sawdust ground,
Who shared the pleasures fierce and fine
Of goblet, schooner, tankard, stein,
Or piped with me what tender tunes
Comprise the saga of saloons,

When, in the advancing summer night,
The men from pits of anthracite
Tramped thunderous through the yielding door
And bought us all a round or more,
While other boys were killing frogs,
Or tying cans to orphan dogs,
Or trampling on the lettuce-beds,
Or breaking windows, doors, and heads,
Or stealing milk and copper wire,
Or setting outhouses on fire,
Or making gentle faces blanch
Of pious Christians (Hebrew branch),
Or tearing linen from the line,
Or filching gadgets from the mine,
Or swiping marbles from the meeker,
Or punching noses of the weaker,
And learning all the paltry tricks
Of trade, finance, and politics—
O playmates of a halcyon day,
What verse (I ask you) could convey
The innocent, the clean, the clear,
The golden comradeship of beer,
When, harmless as a day in June,
We quaffed it in the old saloon?
Stay down, O sad and sunken sun,
While Echo sourly grumbles, "None!"

For children bred in a saloon
Are harmless as a night in June,
And when to Man's estate they grow,
Retain the vernal *status quo*.
They never learn the tawdry tricks
Of trade, finance, or politics,
Or harbor sinister intent
Of one day being President,

[44]

Or Congressman, or Senator,
Ambassador or Governor,
Or Universal Financiers,
Or Other-People's Budgeteers—
But simple as the sunny grass,
They let the cycles come and pass
And sometimes mewingly rehearse
The tricks of tetrametric verse,
Or daub a ship in morning light,
Or mine a bit of anthracite,
Or sit on curbs in urban byways
Or fences on bucolic highways,
Or by romantic melancholy
Freed early from all earthly folly,
Lie peacefully and stare at rain
And tickle roots up into grain.

O Congress, as you hold them dear,
Give the hapless children beer;
Restore their gentle nurse, Saloon,
To keep them simple and immune
From every influence that shapes
Young manhood into adult apes;
From mousy mayhems, cheap assaults,
And other small, felonious faults;
Transmute into a public good
Their picayune delinquenthood,
Their piddling pilfering of cars,
And make them noble men in bars—
If they must show their manhood clear,
Let them knock off the heads of beer,
That to their pristine natures true,
They may not grow to be like you;
Oh, save them from the sallow yield
Of church and school and playing field,

Where (*vide* Duke of Wellington)
Such bays as Waterloo are won,
And the alternate brag and whine
Are neatly tuned to rain and shine,
And, as you hold the future dear,
O Congress, give the children beer!

Progress

PROGRESS

They'll soon be flying to Mars, I hear—
But how do you open a bottle of beer?

A flash will take you from Nome to New York—
But how the hell do you pull a cork?

They'll rocketeer you to Hibernia—
But open a window and get a hernia.

They've stripped space from the widow'd blue—
But where is the lace that fits a shoe?

Where is the key that fits a lock?
Where is the garter that holds a sock?

They'll hop to the moon and skip to the stars,
But what'll stay put are the lids on jars.

The mighty telescope looks far,
But finds no place to park a car.

The world crackles with cosmic minds
Tangled up in Venetian blinds.

One day they'll resurrect the dead,
Who'll die again of colds in the head.

Nocturne: West Los Angeles

NOCTURNE: WEST LOS ANGELES

Faintly tremulous, the night
Exudes her mild and membranous light,
And on the garden's flowery floor
The cat inhales the sycamore,
Sprawls on the parsley, mint or chives,
Felicitous in all his lives,
Or from a comfortable ledge
Views the horizon of a hedge,
Alert, assured, compact, complete,
Poised for aggression or retreat,
Unlicked, save by his own caress
In the neat cause of cleanliness,
At one with all, at peace, at ease
In all his fine felinities—
Surely along some scented sod
He ate that scurrying mouse called God.

Demos is Done

DEMOS IS DONE

Demos is done, the brute that ruled too long,
Spewed tyrants, tended them and made them strong,
Crushed God and good, blocked wisdom's gentle ways,
Spat at the sunrise of evolving days,
Clubbed Truth, made compact with the ancient dead,
That he be safely chained and poorly fed.
Aristos comes to take him by the hand
And weeping Demos waits the mild command,
The roomier collar, bigger bone, clean floor,
The window'd kennel and the sky-blue door.

Flies without Ointment

FLIES WITHOUT OINTMENT

I

I'm Fond of Doctors

I'm fond of doctors and drivers of hacks
Whose names are Morris and Barney and Max;
I'm fond of waiters in places I know
Whose names are Louis and Mike and Joe;
They take my mind off taxes and love—
A very good taking the mind off of.

II

Good Morning, Browning

God's in his heaven
Painting things blue;
I'm on the thorn,
The snail is too.

III

Oral History and Prognostication

One cannot mastic-
Ate with plastic;

Porcelain stains;
Cement pains;
Gold glitters;
Diamond twitters;
Lead sinks;
Iron stinks;
Wood rots;
Coal blots;
Zinc corrodes;
Uranium explodes;
Bridges miss;
Plates hiss;
Copper hums—
Hurrah, gums!

IV

When I Peruse the Journals

When I peruse the journals gray with strife
On earth, and hence assume distress above,
I must conclude, regretfully, that life
Seems (no reflection on the honest wife)
The occupational disease of love.

V

A Couple of Dachshunds

A couple of dachshunds are Sweeney and Joe,
As pleasant companions as any I know;
Their persons are decent, though slightly mephitic;
Their ancestry German, their noses Semitic.

Their appetites frankly are rather Teutonic—
Gargantuan, colossal, immense, mastodonic,
But whatever the faults of the children of Moses,
I am glad that the rest of them followed their noses.

VI

To the Human Rump

Disparaged and derided part,
Disdained by manners, morals, art,
What change in stricken Man's estate
If only you endured its weight—

If hands and head were cast aside,
The claws of greed, the spring of pride,
And till there was no more Begat,
The world sat down and sat and sat!

VII

The Mockingbird

The mockingbird sings in the sycamore tree,
The poplar, the lemon, the willow;
His coloratura exacerbates me
As I pound my anfractuous pillow.

I harbor no prejudice, nourish no gall
For occasional bird singing sweetly,
But exiguous mocking of nothing at all—
I can do that myself, and more neatly.

My sleep is compounded of nightmare and rue;
I toss like a boat on a billow—
Alas, I regret there is nothing to do
But report him to Caesar Petrillo.

VIII

Famous Battle

My lady is lovely as iris or rose,
  Or blossom of apple or cherry;
My feeling for her from her head to her toes
  Is floriverous, fancy, and very.

And yet I regret to confess a distress
  I repress when I can, lest it strike her—
My lovely and lissome and lyrical, yes,
  I love her—but really don't *like* her!

IX

Sad, Mad Song

Love flies out of the window
  When I come in through the door;
When I come in through the window,
  Reverse, and pour—
So, partly serious, but more in jes',
  I try to find rhymes for oranges.

Shepherd Song: 1947

From womb to worm and worm to weed
What does a person really need?—
A million for food and clothes and rent;
A billion for innocent merriment;
A trillion to balance the budget and
A zillion for taxes, to keep on hand;
A zzillion more, and the hillside's dew-pearled,
And what do you think we've got?—One World!
And one can live as cheaply as two—
So what is there really for you to do
But draw the curtain and go to bed
And pull the cover over your head
And lie there warm and well-concealed
And consider the lilies of the field?
Man wants so little here below:
The items listed—the rest is show.

Revelation

REVELATION

In the Evening

Star-bright in the evening,
The apricot blossoms seem to sing,
Sing to the harassed heart and mind
Something infinitely kind,
Something compassionate. I strain
To hear the numbers mild as rain,
To see the sweet tree's flower-kissed
Beneficent evangelist;
And then a word is murmured clear,
Then two, then three caress my ear,
Each fluttering like a candle flame—
And Scotch-and-soda is the name.

In the Morning

My head, which is about to split,
Says Scotch-and-soda wasn't *it*.
So many lesser things are prized
Before a man is civilized,
That only bee and Hottentot
May understand the apricot.

Comparative Survey

COMPARATIVE SURVEY

The camel looks a bit distorted;
The fecund rabbit rather thwarted—
For Nature's laws are sometimes brittle,
Too much bedevils like too little—
The monstrous elephant moronic;
The quilly porcupine platonic;
The exemplary ant, alas,
Seems just a microscopic ass,
Considering how he must pant
And sweat and strive to be an ant;
The eagle has a savage beak
Which none (I hope) presumes to tweak,
Whereas the sparrow, small and shoddy,
Is hissed and boo'd by everybody;
Slick moons on humid summer nights
Promote the primitive delights,
When desperate rich and hopeful poor
Serve that Paris wench *l'amour;*
The river runs into the sea;
The dog into the bustling flea;
The man, tormented and forgot
From birth to earth and who knows what,
Runs into debt, despair and hives,
Needy friends and former wives,
Erosions of the brain and liver
And thence into the Jordan River,

Precisely as he used to do
When Science thought the sky was blue,
And bossy Jahveh thundered through,
And Christ was nothing but a Jew.

The Notebook of a Schnook

THE NOTEBOOK OF A SCHNOOK

schnook=schlemiel

I

I'm sitting home, I feel lonesome,
I feel saber-toothed and ownsome;
If I had a friend of the female gender
I feel I could make the girl surrender.
So I call this one, I call that one,
A bright one, a dim one, a slim one, a fat one,
Till I find a girl who says she's willing
To do the cooing if I do the billing.
So I bill in one place, I bill in another,
And she coos a little, like Whistler's mother;
Then I take her home to my mortgaged chalet,
A cute little place, if not a *palais*,
In a very respectable part of town,
With some rooms upstairs and some down;
I play a record by Tchaikovsky,
A very high-toned approach to lovsky;
I play waltzes by all the Strausses
And name big names in adjoining houses;
I try etchings, book-ends, brandy,
Rare editions and nougat candy,
Broadloom carpet and rose-leaf ceiling,
On which she can look, I hope, with feeling—
And what happens? You won't believe it;
As usual, nothing—take it or leave it!

II

I write a scenario for moving pictures;
I let myself go without any strictures;
My mind works in bright ascensions;
The characters swell and get dimensions;
The heroine rises from Gimbel's basement
To what could be called a magic casement,
By sheer virtue and, call it pluck,
With maybe a reel and a half of luck;
She doesn't use posterior palsy
Or displace so much as a single falsie;
She scorns the usual oo-la-la
And never ruffles a modest bra,
(The censor's dream of the cinema);
She doesn't find pearls in common oysters;
She sips a little but never roisters.
The hero's gonads are under wraps,
He never clutches or cuffs or slaps
In heat Vesuvian, or even Stygian—
He acts Oxonian or Cantabrigian
With maybe a soupçon of the South—
Cotton wouldn't melt in his mouth;
The plot could harmlessly beguile
A William Wordsworth honey chile;
The Big Shot's hot and the little shotlets
Wake their wives with contagious hotlets.
So what happens? The usual factors—
The studio simply can't get actors,
Directors, cutters, stagehands, stages,
Or girls to type the extra pages:
The way it ends, to put it briefly,
Is what happens is nothing, chiefly.

I work hard, I earn little,
A roof, a beer, a vittle, a skittle;
I keep—well what, if you haven't got money
Do you *think* you can keep—a high-class honey,
Maybe a nobleman's youngest daughter
With a yacht to protect her from salt and water?—
I keep a budget, a can of herring,
A box of matzos and maybe swearing.
Well, the worm turns 'round like a fresh-made cruller,
He's now a horse of another color—
I begin to make money, fast and plenty;
Life looks like rainbows and spumenti;
I begin to regard Jehovah highly,
And think of the life of the younger Riley;
I begin to dream of Lucullan doin's:
I'll travel a lot and see the ruins;
I'll hire a butler who doesn't hurry,
Who doesn't work, but who's pure Surrey,
A chauffeur who looks like the late Lord Essex,
A maid with wattles firm and Wessex;
I'll pay, spot cash, three years' advance
And import a cook from Paris, France;
O Paris, France! O Town de luxe!
I see you as you were in books—
O Paris, France, where gay *les femmes*
Cavort and do not give a *demmes;*
Where waxed and debonair *les hommes*
Disport and do not give a *dommes;*
Where even merry *les enfants*
Know all and do not give a *dants!*—
I'm running wild, I must subdue
What you could call my parvenu—

Well anyhow, I'm thinking of
La belle amour and even love;
Of serving dinners in ten courses,
And meeting gents who own horses
And powerful, natural female forces
Who own the gents who own the horses—
So what happens? I pay taxes;
The earth wobbles on half an axis;
I'm happy if the butler's cousin
Drops in sometimes for a daily dozen,
If I meet people who fix plumbing,
Or own a goldfish that's up and coming—
Things could happen to guys like Nero,
But to me, excuse the expression, zero.

IV

I paid my taxes. I got sick;
The doctor said I was going quick
Of double multiple complications,
Confirmed by seven consultations.
Well, if this is it, I said, resigned,
I'll do some thinking in my mind,
I'll do some planning in my head
On the way I'll live when they say I'm dead.
Well, first I'll go and get my blessing,
Then take my time about convalescing,
Because the sickness that I got
Weakens a fellow quite a lot.
I'll lie around a couple of eons
And listen to them pealing paeans
And drumming on what they call there, tabors,
And get acquainted with the neighbors,

And flop and sprawl on golden grass
And watch the little cherubs pass,
The way, up there, they call their cuties—
And from the pictures are they beauties!—
Sift pearls and rubies through my fingers,
Sing tenor with the carol singers,
And while I'm loafing, maybe lay
Some onyx up for a rainy day.
Then when I'm feeling good and strong
And think that I can live that long—
Because up there you feel immortal
Or else they show you the so-called portal—
I'll move into my permanent mansion,
With grounds enough for later expansion,
Take a look-see 'round the place,
Pick up a little special grace,
Meet the Biggies, make my mark,
Get promoted from angel to arch-,
Or maybe, even this could be,
To seraph, thirty-third degree,
With extra wings. Well, that's about
As far as I got when I passed out.
So what happened? To put it clearly,
Not only nothing, but nothing merely
And absolutely. You won't believe it:
I'm not even an angel—take it or leave it.

Mild Observation

MILD OBSERVATION

When Genghis Khan, for bloody robe,
Wore one-half the flowing globe,
Nations trembled at his tread
And envied their completed dead.

Now Genghis is a misty name
But mentioned when the young declaim,
And even later horrors seem
Dissolving vapors of a dream.

A little horror now and then
Seems relished by the world of men,
Else, how could it so soon prepare
For newer horrors in the air.

To Joyce Kilmer, Respectfully

TO JOYCE KILMER, RESPECTFULLY

"Poems are made by fools like me,
But only God can make a tree"—
So what can fools like me essay
Who cannot make a night or day,
A star, a herring, or a worm,
A mountain or a modest germ,
A lily, lamb, or even fleece,
Or, like the Lord Himself, a peace,
A zephyr or a hurricane,
A zebra, antelope, or rain;
Who cannot even fashion pain?

While God was busy with His tree,
Who made the fools like you and me?
Did He assign some lesser god
To shape us of inferior sod?
Did we slip through some secret door
While branches strewed His workroom floor?

To many, who but dimly see,
Your poem made a flowering tree,
And did not Jesus by Siloam
Make of gentle words a poem
Whereof a tree was born in light
Upon a man's astonished sight?

To a Certain Person

TO A CERTAIN PERSON

Within this room we have identity—
God's mark and manumission. Here, no bleak
Fusion of each with all, that none is free.
Here we have self—raped word by which the weak
Exorcise life. Assurance, young and strong,
Walks tall and tender, arm in arm with fate.
Figures emerge from the sweet womb of song.
Here I behold and blithely recreate
Hellenic evenings in your garnet hair.
Here nights, rich-tasting, every hunger slake.
Songs gush from rock. And in this room we dare,
In spite of totems and taboos, to make
The livid world and its factitious doom
A bright extension of this little room.

The Complete Works
of Josiah Hopestone

I

Boy

The boy is told to be a man. But why?
For strength, why not the elephant or ox?
The eagle for assurance in the sky?
For grace, the tiger, speed, the hound or fox?

For courage not compact of serried mass
Why not the lion, and the hare for love?
For fortitude the philosophic ass?
For innocence why not the deer or dove?

For patience and humility, the horse?
For publicized distinctiveness, the gnu?
For faith, and will to make of faith a force,
Why not a woman, and for wisdom too?

For peace, why not an oyster or a clam?
For pleasure in his trade, why not a bee?
For some sweet Mary's sake, why not a lamb?
And almost anything for honesty?

The boy is malleable; he may weave
These elements into a noble span—
Is it not said we are what we believe?
Then why this vile and venal thing called man?

Or, if the task be easier, for joy,
Why not adjure him to remain a boy?

II

Air for the G-String

The bawdy and busy-ast
Buxom ecdysiast
Grinds and bumps
Her hinter-humps.

The equally asinine
Quasi-masculine
Is delighted
And excited.

And why not?
Sterile motion, sterile deed
And fruitless seed.
Here is his story better told
Than by harsh days of heat and cold.

III

Wanted

Wanted—by Dayrise and rosiferous Earth,
By Noon and Afternoon and Evening,
By Trees, Hedges, Bushes, Birds, Grass,
By Justice, and What-Good-May-Come-to-Pass,
By the Solar System, Stellar Universe,
A Person missing in Recorded Time,
Sole Heir of the Sublime,

For the return of these, his Properties,
Now in their keeping—
His Rights, his Mind, Identity and Soul,
Also, his Obligations.

Occupation:
For Battle—
Cattle;
For Peace—
Fleece;
For Life—
Servant of Mass and Myth, Hewer of Hollow Stones;
For Death—
Bones.

Name: Individual Man.

IV

Metamorphosis

I used to breathe unexcised air,
Ensorcelled by Circean care,
As bilious, choleric and glum
As folk possessed by Kingdom Come.
Suburbia on a Sunday night
Was not a more forbidding sight—
My brow was creased, my pants were not;
I horrified the cradled tot;
I let my whiskers grow in reams
To thwart the barber in his themes,
And gloated when my stubborn fleece
Annulled his conversation piece;

I glowered at the passerby,
Pooh-pooh'd the sea, the stars, the sky,
Was wont in malice to reflect
With *double entendre, mot* direct,
On roses, robins, hip or breast,
Or anything these might suggest,
And once, with sour and cynic quips,
Refused to look at an eclipse.

And then one night, when I was filled
With thaumaturgic grain, distilled,
Bottled, uncorked, and poured in glass,
A transformation came to pass,
A metamorphosis was wrought
By this horrendous dread and thought:
When my stenotic days were over
My bones would turn to poisoned clover,
Arsenic grass, unfit to chew,
A noxious nut, or maybe two,
Which trusting sparrow, squirrel and cow
Would eat, and say farewell to Now,
Would shuffle off their mortal slips
Because I snubbed a fine eclipse,
Because I was a grouse, a grump,
A churl, a heel, a cad, a chump.
How should I face my honest friends
When Gabriel called to dividends
And all of us together rose
And entered heaven, nose by nose?
My pores ran wild, my hair stood up—
I felt a dirty buttercup.

Now, when my fellow men dismay
Themselves, the earth, and night and day,

And I could look with merry quips
Upon their permanent eclipse,
Or when Jehovah, Jove, or Zeus
Decides I am a cornered moose,
I think of cows upon the munch
Or happy sparrows having lunch
Or furry squirrels at their brunch,
And radiate, effuse, exude,
And even sweat the cheerful mood,
And loose my dentures in a smile,
And walk a lissome quarter-mile,
And say hello to tots and nurses,
And mull some amiable verses,
And do not think of folk I pass
As noxious nuts or poisoned grass.

I wish there were a conscious movement
Among the beasts for our improvement.

V

Derivative Quatrain
Discovered on a Wall of the Author's Attic

Tax me not in mournful numbers,
Come and make a total haul,
For the residue that slumbers
Is no good to me at all.

VI

Potential Menace, cooing in your Crib,
For all I know, the Embryonic Fib,
The Nascent Whopper or Rococo Word
By which to hypnotize the Ovine Herd,
Now in liquescent Diaper strait confined,
But possibly for Leadership designed,
For Head or Tail or Maw or Claw of State,
Rehearsing now to lie or liquidate,
Harass, confuse, betray, appeal or beg—
My Minatory Twig, my Serpent Egg,
Rockabye. . . .

VII

Balmy Ooze with Bryophytes

The hippopotamus delights
In balmy ooze with bryophytes,
Whereon he lolls and sprawls and snoozes
And, being one with Nature, oozes,
Snorting a lush and mighty breath
And seeming unprepared for death,
While Man, serenity eschewing,
Is always up and down and doing,
For aqueous days a painful sieve,
Equipped to die but not to live.
Sadly I weigh the hippo's gains
Against my few and scattered brains,

His hide against my shirt and pants,
His fleas against my massive ants,
And choose the ooze and water-plants.

VIII

Song for the Flute

O, dear familiar of my heart,
So gracious, fair and kind,
Would you could lose your other part
Of stranger to my mind.

O, would that Reason were as blind
As Love, or had the art
Of seeming pleasantly resigned,
Or feigning the fierce dart.

From deserts of the wise I start
Toward You, my love, and find
The dearest substance of my heart,
A shadow of my mind.

IX

Thorn Song

Talent in evil
Ends on the gallows,
But genius in evil
Avoids the shallows,
Rides currents high and free
And fashions heroes for humanity.

[103]

X

Wilderness

The wilderness which only storms caress,
Seas from the living world a void apart,
May drain a deeper, icier loneliness
Out of the human heart.

XI

Question and Answer

What is so rare as a day in June?
Decent behavior
From a popular savior.

"It Is Finished"

"IT IS FINISHED"

He said, It is finished: and He bowed
His Head and gave up the ghost. John 19:30

No, Lord, it is not finished. You are still
Transfixed upon the wood, the world your hill;
The spear has lengthened to the branching spire;
The crown become humanity on fire,
Burning Your brow with fiercer pain than thorn,
With hate more piercing than the Roman scorn.
The mourners at Your feet are very few.
It is not finished, till a sunrise new
Strike from the minds of men the wounds that bleed,
And leave them gasping at the Word, the Deed.

For a Zither

FOR A ZITHER

These things are eternally true
To the memory of you:
An empty vase that held your rose,
Books that only you may close,
Doors that let you go, whose wood
Is wistful with my solitude,
A lonely lamp with shade awry,
As if it struggled not to cry,
As if some shade-born hope said "wait,"
And you would come to set it straight.
The very silence 'round these things
Of a remembered motion sings,
Motion you gave to them and grace
And in our heaven their starry place:
These things kept the vows we made,
These things were true, and we betrayed.

Churchbells

CHURCHBELLS

When I was a little lad
Sunday churchbells made me sad,
Made me wish I hadn't been
Born a Jew and deep in sin,
For as many a Christian boy
Told me with unChristly joy
I had personally done
A thing to blacken sky and sun,
In hate and malice sacrificed
His Lord and Saviour, Jesus Christ,
And though, since I was barely ten,
I couldn't quite remember when
I had done the hellish thing,
I used to hear the churchbells ring,
And dogs of terror scampered blind
Through Ghetto alleys of my mind,
And barked in bells from Christian spires,
And ran in rings 'round Christian fires,
And crucifixes, wild of eye,
On their single legs strode by.

I watched the people, still and strange,
Passing in their Sunday change,
Knife-lipped women, rock-faced men,
Seemingly the same as when

I saw them every other day,
Yet skies and seas and lands away,
And felt forlorn and child-alone,
And felt that way among my own—
No Gentile dark with love of Christ
Whom I and mine had sacrificed,
No Jew with skullcap on his head
Mumbling something Moses said—
A leaf that fluttered from no tree,
Nor came to rest, nor yet was free,
A tree that walked, but never grew,
A living semblance, but a Jew,
Lost in the United States,
Lost behind the Ghetto gates,
No bird, yet wingless, lost in air,
Alone and alien everywhere.

Now I am a large and mellow,
Mild and philosophic fellow
Of amiable thought and speech,
Sweetly disposed toward all and each,
A stanch disciple of Saint Paul,
A friend of sparrows as they fall,
Contained, reflective and resigned,
Of equable Franciscan mind,
Content with almost anything,
I hear the Sunday churchbells ring
Upon a morning broad and bright,
And think the little lad was right
And *will* be till the gods unite
And One God says, "Let there be light!"

Stanzas

STANZAS

The hoptoad hops from here to there
And then from there to here,
If he has business anywhere
He does not make it clear,
And yet, I notice, when he stops
He seems intent on further hops.

A purpose surely lies in these
Concatenated jumpings,
Divine, as in the buzzing bee's
Persistent flower-thumpings;
Or up, of course, a few gradations,
The hoppy history of nations.

Weather Report

WEATHER REPORT

I

Freudian Footnote

I love my love because she's fair
And has a cold-wave in her hair;
Because her lips and handbags match
And she's considered quite a catch;
Because she has the winsome ways
Of waiters in the best cafés;
Dependable as Holland gin,
I always know whose bed she's in,
So purely flustered when she lies,
Three times I've doubted my own eyes;
Because she listens with a look
Of violets by a babbling brook,
As bright and beautiful as they,
As sensitive to what I say—
But most, this shiny suit I press
Because for *me* I care much less.

II

Emendation

When lovely woman stoops to rise
In furs and jewels to the eyes,
Call it any kind of folly,
You cannot make her melancholy!

III

Thought While Serving on a Jury

When I was young in that green time
Between B.C. and now,
And rhymed to live and lived to rhyme
And loved the girls like chow,
And thoughts of what I *couldn't* get
Disturbed not what I got,
And life was like the alphabet,
Why, I was young—so what?

IV

Parlor Game

Who pays and pays and pays? The woman!
Humanly frail, divinely human!
Who pays the woman? The paying teller!
Who pays the teller? Oh, just some feller!

V

The Forest of Arden

An epoch writhes and dies,
But in the nightclubs and shops
The glamor-girls glitter and twitter
And peck at slops.

VI

For the Harmonica

When in course of time you see,
In place of an illusion, me,
Please remember that you cozen'd
Me into the man I wasn't.

He, by that time, being dead,
Give your heart to me, instead;
You may find, to your surprise,
A faint resemblance in the eyes!

VII

Soliloquy While Waiting

Never let your passion rise
To your head or to the skies;
Confine it to protective pants
Along with sundry other ants;
A cheerier world, a greener earth
Is bought with, say, three buttons' worth.

VIII

Composed on the Beach at Santa Monica

Constant as the climate,
Fickle as the weather,
We shall be eternally,
Capriciously together.

Song for Election Day

Winter, or spidery Spring,
Summer, or cidery Fall,
Whatever my fortune may bring,
Je suis un derrière du cheval.

Do not too hastily spring
Therefore, poor *me* to condemn;
Whatever *your* fortune may bring—
Tu, mon ami, es le même.

Drums

DRUMS

Lying in the dark I hear,
Shaken with wonder, cold with fear,
The tiny drumbeats of my heart
Play their incessant, fatal part.

Two billion hearts, by day and night,
Drum down the shade, drum up the light,
Drum seasons up to tend the tree,
Drum strength and sound into the sea,
Drum Death out of Eternity.

The Forest

THE FOREST

You cast the deed so lightly on the stream
Of Time, and think it lightly flows away;
You cast the word so lightly to the day,
These pledges that you never can redeem
If at some fatal moment in the scheme
Of life you may have need of them again—
The deed that might have sheltered you from pain,
The word that might have saved another's dream.
You are no solitary tree that stands
And drops its leaves upon a barren place,
But one whose leaves and branches interlace
A multitude with living hearts and hands:
The same life sings in you that sings in these,
And babbles of immense antiquities.

Mid-May Song

MID-MAY SONG

Now mid-May's here and I contrive
To add two twos and make them five.
Meanwhile, the loud, mammalian earth
Imbues with her priapic mirth
The hippopotamus and flea,
The queer baboon, the cruising bee,
The caterpillar on the tree,
The proud giraffe (who knows that he
Is modern architecturally)—
Imbues, in short, with springtime all
The Kingdom of the Animal,
Save one, whose maladjusted span
Constitutes the Life of Man.

While birds toot sweet on every bough,
And grass-grown yearnings fill the cow
With milk (grade A), and even cream,
And things are maybe what they seem,
And chickens, tipsy with the May,
Lay and lay and lay and lay
And lay (lay off; go on from here!)
And jolly mid-May flies appear,
In perfect harmony with all
On which they chance to light or fall,
And more successful upside down

Than any leading man in town—
While this occurs, and even more,
From shore to (naturally) shore,
And tick and tiger, bee and bear
Make vernal whoopee everywhere,
The lord of Science and the Arts,
Self-sung for various noble parts—
No less than Man himself I mean—
Continues to perplex the scene
And make the startled spring go boom
With antic gesta hominum;
With isms, schisms, cults and creeds;
With febrile itches, phantom needs;
With saws and laws and cant and prayer;
With graft and craft and greed and care;
With freakish use and monster skill;
With idiot goal and maniac will;
With spires and swords and leagues and wars
And surfs of talk on sandy shores;
With in hoc signo on a Sunday
And caveat emptor, starting Monday;
With sour achieving, harried striving,
Belly pacts and spleen conniving,
With—halt! survey the dimpled sight,
And catalogue your own delight.

Of all who labored from the slime
Under the dogged feet of Time,
While past slipped into crackling past,
Is this, is Man, the first or last?
Has not the ape contrived to reach
Beyond the barren buttes of speech,
Beyond the quicksands of the mind
(His serio-comic world behind),

A pride, a place, a peace more stanch
In his plain Heaven of a branch?
Has not the tree itself attained
Its topmost powers, and stands ordained
In priesthood of harmonious place?
Before it found an equal grace,
What conquered worlds behind the bird
Of cactus Deed and tidal Word?
Is not, most ancient of the stock,
The rock melodious to the rock
Of human woes and human pains
Remembered in its empty veins?
Is there no wisdom wiser than
The fret, the fear, the whine of Man?

Well, mid-May's here and I contrive
To add two twos and keep alive,
And ponder Plato, now a fly,
Upon his ceiling of a sky.

Song, on Reading That the Cyclotron Has Produced Cosmic Rays, Blasted the Atom into Twenty-two Particles, Solved the Mystery of the Transmutation of Elements and Devil Knows What

SONG, ON READING THAT THE CYCLOTRON
HAS PRODUCED COSMIC RAYS, BLASTED
THE ATOM INTO TWENTY-TWO PARTICLES,
SOLVED THE MYSTERY OF THE TRANS-
MUTATION OF ELEMENTS AND DEVIL
KNOWS WHAT

Be gay, be merry, and don't be wary of milking the
    modest minute;
Rollick and frolic and carpe diem for all the fun
    that's in it;
Gather roses, or rose-red noses, and samba the night
    away:
There's nothing to fear but life and death—as far
    as we know today.

The lads in the lab are in high confab and the gods
    are huddled in holes;
There's a murmuration of trepidation among estab-
    lished souls;
The atom's groggy, the future foggy, so join your
    doggie at play:
There's nothing to fear but life and death—as far
    as we know today.

There's rootin' and tootin' in stellar spaces and secret
    places therein;
The mild professors are now possessors of something
    stronger than gin;

Before the payoff let's take a layoff and all be queens
of the May:
There's nothing to fear but life and death—*as far
as we know today!*

Rhymed Observations

RHYMED OBSERVATIONS

The rights of each are the only rights of all.

Eve grinned before the fall.

The malevolent tyrant destroys; the benevolent tyrant humiliates.

Man proposes; woman affiliates.

Wherever the worm turns, he is still a worm.

Power never serves too brief a term.

Where there are willing masters there are willing slaves.

Where there are mass men there are mass graves.

Only the obligations of the strong assure the rights of the weak.

Envy is the mistress of the meek.

Marriages made in Heaven are not exported.

A fool and his money are soon courted.

[147]

When the ox has wings, the eagle will draw the cart.

The taste of another's luck is always tart.

Who shouts of his labor covets another's yield.

What God confided to the clergy has never been revealed.

A wrong to one outlaws the State.

Free to worship still means free to hate.

Where the mighty swarm, God is hidden.

Joy is the most forbidden.

Real wealth is the soul in repose.

Thorns do not impede the rose.

Where one is nothing, all are nothing.

Beware of a dog and a saviour frothing.

"No" is a giant's word.

Parents should be seen, but children heard.

The body cannot give itself pleasure.

Work is the fig-leaf of leisure.

Who governs himself cheats the State.

[148]

Faith condones, Courage despises, Fate.

The wages of sin are high.

The half-truth is the cancer of the lie.

Every man's poverty adds to the demagogue's wealth.

Few reach high office save by stealth.

The lying servant becomes the brutal master.

Only One God is not made of plaster.

No taxation without misrepresentation.

Geography never made a nation.

Who robs Peter will never pay Paul.

The thirst of the great is the drink of the small.

The wealth of the world will be redistributed with its brains.

To starve more slowly, starve on another's gains.

No man should be called common except by his cook.

We need more cooks.

No man is fit, by law or wit, or custom, suffrage or intent, or hazard, need or accident, to rule another than himself, save from the gallows or the shelf.

Wisdom bears buds, Virtue, blossoms, Force, fruit.

On the hog mind, assurance is the snoot.

To a woman, experience means love; to a man, traffic tickets.

Simple Saint Peter stays outside the wickets, knowing, as *he* does, by his own belief, the stinkweed has become immortal leaf, and the starved mind and heart eternal rickets.

So long—and yet, so short, for this life's grievance and the snort.

Old Testament

OLD TESTAMENT

I

Moses

Below him Canaan glittered like a shield;
He saw the land beneath the burning sun
And dreamed its milk and honey field by field:—
Not bitterly he knew his work was done
And laid in misty Death's that mighty hand.
He sat upon a rock and gazed; the Lord,
Standing beside him, spake: "Behold, the land
That I have promised unto Joshua's sword,
Unto my children, Israel, for a crown!"
He gazed on Canaan and he shed no tears—
The burden of his people weighed him down;
The weariness of all those desert years.
He smiled a little before he fell asleep
Thinking how he had sowed and who shall reap.

II

Joshua

"Moses, my servant, is dead." So spake the Lord,
Laying a hand all warm with love and sun
Upon the shoulders of the son of Nun,
"And I shall keep with thee my promised Word!"
And Joshua fumbled at his girded sword,

For on his arm the hand of Israel's God
Was trembling like a grass-blade in the sod.
The mighty Captain plucked his garment's cord,
And dared not look upon the Face that spake,
Hearing a Voice that wavered like a flame
Before the mention of His servant's name.
He thought the Heart of God would surely break,
And looked out tearfully upon his clan;
The Lord of Wrath was weeping like a man.

To a Friend, B.J., Age, Six Months

TO A FRIEND, B.J., AGE, SIX MONTHS

Hello, Fats!
Hello, Smiler!
Four-bottle Man and Unaware Beguiler!
Philosopher without philosophy;
No prophet, but Incarnate Prophecy
Of something hunky-dory and okay
That's on the way
And will arrive one day, or any day!
I seem to see you wink an eye,
Bump a shoulder against the sky
Confidentially,
As if to say, *"They'll* see."
Hello, you Dimpled Future, Shriver of the Past,
Recaster of all things miscast,
Sayer—I hear you, though no word is said,
No sign, save a small rumple on the bed
And sundry hollows—
Of this, as follows:
"We are not shaped for grief or hate or wrong,
But fruitful labor, happy love and song
And innocence and fellowship and joy."
Hello, Boy!
You, who are still with sunrise, answer this:
What's gone amiss?
Aha—I see; I'm sure I saw you nod
Again, as follows: "We ourselves, not God—

And God another name for what we are,
Not something far beyond the farthest star."
Well, thanks, Fats!
Thanks, Smiler!
Real Wise Guy!
Small Beguiler!

Personal Notation

PERSONAL NOTATION

At night, when you *should* sleep, you can't sleep yet;
By day, when you shouldn't, you laugh at sheep yet;
Things you're expecting, they get aphasia;
Things you're avoiding fly over from Asia;
If you want to go out, you could tear your hair yet,
You could even break dishes, and not think where yet;
If you want to stay in, a dozen people
Bang at the phone like bats in a steeple;
If you feel fine, from toe to cranium
You look like a relic of Herculaneum;
If you feel sick, you look sturdy—
So what will the end be? Well, where is Verdi?

If you like a girl, she likes biceps,
Regular he-men and even triceps,
Which you don't get from wrestling verses
Or playing checkers with night nurses;
If you meet a girl whom God forgot yet,
She wants to protect you from Heaven knows what
    yet;
If you want to cavort and sing and laugh yet,
The party's a meeting of Chiefs of Staff yet;
If you feel the way a mortician looks yet,
They get so gay they drag in the cooks yet;
Loafers eat while you stay broke yet—
So what will the end be? Ask James K. Polk yet!

If you like birds, you'll live in New York yet,
Where children arrive without even a stork yet;
If you think a lark is a loud-mouthed weevil,
You're sure to commute to a forest primeval;
If you want a world at least as bearable
As it was in the time of Ivan the Terrible,
They begin to prepare for a deadlier war yet
To exterminate all, and even more yet;
If you feel relaxed at such release yet,
They turn around and threaten peace yet—
So what will the end be? Well, read the papers
In a million years, and compare the capers.

A Simple Tale

A SIMPLE TALE

I had a girl and *you* had a girl
And she was a pretty dame,
And mine was mine and yours was yours
And she was one and the same.

Yes, *I* had a girl and *you* had a girl
And she had a lovely laugh,
And whenever *I* saw her, whenever *you* saw her,
We always sawed her in half.

Now *she* has a fellow, a loving fellow,
But a careworn fellow and pale,
Who wonders which of us got the head
And which of us got (a simple tale),
And which of us got the other part,
And which of us got, in short, her heart.

Practical Conclusion

PRACTICAL CONCLUSION

This is the better way for us, my dear,
This pleasant and convenient compromise;
I should have lost you had you seen me clear
With innocent or unremembering eyes.

But, as it is, substantially I please,
Observed, while some subconscious dream abets,
Through stained-glass windows of your memories,
Or camellia-mists of your subdued regrets.

Obituary

OBITUARY

When a body is broken
Something is shaken
From all things that are—
A face, a garden, a God, a star.

The sun will not be less
In strength, or night in tenderness;
They will be just as flawless, just as fair,
But something that was there will not be there.

The moon will be as shimmering and as bright
As when, on one vast, sea-receding night,
She taught the nascent eye to utter light.

But she will know in her mercurial soul
That she is not as whole.

For I was one string on a dulcimer
That sang her radiant beauty back to her.
My eye that held her majesty was seen
In dark she could not enter, being queen.

For each holds the stars in their courses
And each holds a God on His throne,
And the life that goes into darkness
Always takes back its own.

Fantasy on a Familiar Theme

FANTASY ON A FAMILIAR THEME

I shot an arrow into the air,
It fell to earth and I knew where;
It fell like a plummet, swift and free,
Into the U.S. Treasury.

I breathed a song into the air
And thought it would find a landing there;
But down it went, like a skiff at sea,
Into the U.S. Treasury.

I tossed my labor into the air
To scatter the crows of fear and care;
Down it came, but not to me—
Into the U.S. Treasury.

I threw a statesman into the air;
The world and weather changed to fair;
But down he dropped, like a drunken bee,
Into the U.S. Treasury.

I hurled the Treasury into the air;
I blasted it while it hovered there;
I muttered a prayer, I said a grace—
And there it stood in the same old place.

Advice to the Lovelorn
(Women only)

ADVICE TO THE LOVELORN
(WOMEN ONLY)

Great oaks from little acorns grow;
Ah, would in life the rule were so!
What has the little acorn got
That papa's eager seed has not?

Before the cracking nations fail,
The acorn must supplant the male;
Before the world goes up in smoke,
Ladies, get yourselves with oak!

Quatrain

QUATRAIN

The night climbs upward toward the eternal past;
The silence gnaws at the silent heart like a mouse;
Patience! After so many deaths the last
Is only the locking of an empty house.

Quiz

QUIZ

Do you now refer to fun as folly,
Enjoy night-rising and melancholy?
Is your mind vague and uninspired?
Is your sense of integer vitae tired?
Do your legs ache, does your memory creak?
Do you work an hour and rest a week?
Do you sit in the sun when you should be swimmin'?
Does your middle suggest a ripe persimmon?
Are you glad I didn't rhyme swimmin' with women?)
Do you snort, eruct and sound alarming
When you want to be urbane and charming?
Do you read tales of wild adventure
While you try to dock a floating denture?
Do you absently reach for your noble dome
And find you're holding a useless comb?
Do you have symptoms—spots, itches,
No sense of shame without your britches?
Do you store milk, bicarb of soda
Instead of Scotch in your front pagoda?
Do you look at your wife and remember clearly
That for thirty years you've loved her dearly
With never a twitch for any other,
Pat her shoulder and call her mother?
Well, think of all that was before,
The call to arms in peace or war,

The dates, the parties, jobs and worry,
The itch for sports and scampering hurry,
The haircuts, shaves, shampoos and shines,
The pressings, postures, smirks and lines,
The being alert and still on guard
To win a word or brief regard,
The smoking torches that you carried
Before and after you were married,
The envy, jealousy, fear and spite,
The morning after the maudlin night,
The urgings, purgings, scourgings of
The tender mind in life and love,
And if you're not content with what
You've got, you may think you're old—you're not;
You're full of cold and half-baked beans;
You're in your demi- and semi-teens;
You're quasi-nubile and baby-fat—
And you've got something there, at that.

To a Cat

TO A CAT

If Peace and Silence could arise
And walk, and look with living eyes,
And Night her starry cross descend
And stretch herself and be my friend
For shrimps and beef—I'm certain that
They'd be yourself, imperial cat!

You shame of all your jungle sires,
Of tiger-lords and panther-squires,
Well may these mighty warriors spare
To my distress your royal air—
I to my species, you to theirs
Apostate in adjoining chairs.

Here in this quiet room we dream
Amendments to the primal scheme:
You in your feline terms, of ease,
Catnip, and such urbanities;
I, of a jungle strength to dare to
Smite the three-score ills I'm heir to!

Who Grope, with Love for Hands

WHO GROPE, WITH LOVE FOR HANDS

Who grope, with love for hands, outstretched to light,
Will break their fumbling fingers on a wall.
In that fierce flash of pain the wise see all—
The nested robin and the nested sea,
The silent brood-hen of Eternity,
Marbled in azure that nor speaks nor sings—
And nest their souls beneath those flightless wings.

Portrait

PORTRAIT

Nothing is quite so much in clover
As ancient dames, who grandly sit,
Broad in the beam and beam all over,
At one with every bit of it.

They love assorted nephews, nieces,
Cousins of immemorial date;
The world around them goes to pieces—
But hour by hour they integrate.

And one day they will see Death hover
About the door respectfully,
And, as they would a timid lover,
Wave him in for cakes and tea.

Description

DESCRIPTION

You are no compromise with any dream;
You and the violent world, the actual sun,
The vivid sea, the racing quinquereme,
Struggle, defeat and victory are one.

You are no unguent for diseased regrets,
Those stricken sparrows with the broken wings;
Hermaphrodite of shabby violets
Hid in the attics of forgotten springs.

You are no pale, compensatory shape
That haunts the porch of the surrendered soul;
No dim, nocturnal alley of escape;
No far mirage the wretched call a goal.

No dream that was, no vision that might be
Can decimate your strong reality.

Postlude

POSTLUDE

The next world war was over and done and so was
    the human race;
The stag at bay was at bay no more as he lolled in his
    rilly place;
The pigeon strolled in the rubble heaps with assured
    and easy air,
Or stopped for a chat with a jungle cat or a word with
    a loafing bear.

There was peace at last in the animal world, there was
    peace in the fishful sea;
There was peace on earth, there was peace in time,
    there was peace in Eternity;
The tree was free of the pain of the axe, the earth of
    the pain of the plough,
And she smiled as she suckled the stalwart steer, the
    deer, the sheep and the cow.

It was pleasant indeed when the sun went down and
    the animals walked the sod,
And the birds flew forth and the fish leaped up for
    an evening chat with God,
And the young moon twinkled merrily and glimmered
    a silver glee:
"How nice it is to shine upon such elegant company!"

It was pleasant indeed when the sun came up and the
    animals stirred the sod,
And the parrot rode on the camel's back for a morn-
    ing word with God,
And the young sun twinkled merrily and glimmered a
    golden glee:
"How nice it is to shine upon such charming com-
    pany!"

For the Lord Himself came down for a walk, smok-
    ing a blue cigar,
And the end of it twinkled contentedly, like the morn-
    ing and evening star;
He said "hello" to the eagle and mole and the animals
    far and near,
And the whale and the bass swam close to shore and
    stood on their tails to hear.

He leaned against the firmament and He didn't look
    Big at all;
He looked like all that there was to see, and that can
    be very small;
He leaned against the firmament and threw His cigar
    away,
And the hawk swooped down and the sparrow up, to
    hear what He had to say.

"Well, folks," He said, as He shook His head and
    paused for a zephyr breath,
"The Pest that pestered us One and all has pestered
    himself to death;
It wasn't *My* Will that did him in, it wasn't *My* High
    Command,
For, whatever it was, the Thing I made has long been
    out of Hand.

"You lived in beautiful amity with Me, and each with
  each,
Until I set the Creature down upon the primal beach;
I wasn't quite sure what the Thing might be, when
  first I set him free,
For this was a new experiment in Heavenly Chemistry.

"There was one part I and one part you and a part
  that came to Me,
In a dream that lasted a million years, of a new
  Eternity,
And I wondered whether I could or couldn't, and
  then I resolved I could—
But I didn't know My Chemistry as well as the Good
  Lord should.

"Now you are folks I am glad I made, for all of you
  came out clear:
I never mistook a moose for a mouse or a hornèd toad
  for a deer;
I knew you all by sight and smell and stripe and
  beak and fur,
And I knew how to rule and regulate, for I knew
  what your natures were.

"But This was Something that wasn't you and I'm
  sure that he wasn't I;
He didn't seem to belong on land, in water or air or
  sky;
He fought, bewildered, confused, corrupted My crea-
  tures of soil and sea;
He blocked and battled, dismayed, confused, and cer-
  tainly baffled Me.

"I tried to contain him with threats and gifts, to control and appease and abate;
He left Me no time to evolute *you* to a more enlightened state;
He taught you to trample by his example the laws of the Ought and Must—
Well, I've chalked him down in devil red in column B for Bust.

"But part of his fault was *My* Own Fault, and part of his want and woe,
So part of his dust will be quiet dust and part of the peace you know;
The young who died with unsweetened mouths I will make into honey-bees,
And the fragrant children who never lived shall be my lilac trees.

"I will make an acre of earth and time of the simple, the humble, the good,
And let them utter their whiteness forth in the white of the birchen wood;
And those who wanted only to sing, their death is a piercing wrong:
I will make of their dust a peachtree switch that they find their spring of song.

"I will make of some a rememberance like a voiceless voice in the night;
And some I will keep in My eyes forever and make them part of My sight;
Of the rest I will make a Never Was and turn them out of My Past;
I will turn them into a Dream again—a Bigger Dream than the last."

He stopped and stepped with a single stride into the
massive blue;
The heron stood on a single leg as he does in the evening slough;
The whale remained on his mighty tail, where the
tangled tide was caught;
The tall giraffe leaned on a palm, and thought and
thought and thought.

There was peace at last in the animal world, there
was peace in the fishful sea;
There was peace on earth, there was peace in time,
there was peace in Eternity;
There was peace in the East and peace in the West
and peace in the cobalt span;
There was peace at last in the fading ruins, and peace
in the heart of Man.

To My Mother

TO MY MOTHER

O Mother, with the beautiful, still eyes
These many years dissolved into the earth,
Who never ceased to give my being birth,
You cannot see now from your crumbled grave,
Or through the eyes of the dispassionate stars,
How little even your tenderness could save
My own life from the doom of all men's lives.
Or did you, in the long night silentness
Foresee it all, and weep, that for your love
You took me from the realm of the unborn,
And set me, with a kiss and with a tear,
Upon the road that all men walk with Christ
Unto the thorns, the nails, the rending spear?

Eclogue

ECLOGUE

My heart leaped up when I beheld
A friend of mine named Katzenfeld,
A man as simple as a dish
Of ham and eggs or chips and fish,
Or a geranium in a pot,
Or the unbaptized Hottentot,
Or gentle hiccups gently rumpling
The dreams of the ingested dumpling,
Or Brooklyn as it is today,
Or shining farmers making hay,
Or slanting orchards in the rain,
Or slanting wenches in champagne,
Or Russians rumbling *ochi chornya*
By swimming pools in California,
Or cuties gazing on a book
With long, Laodicean look,
Or sparrows nibbling at a lawn,
Or pigeons gargling up the dawn,
Or lovely ladies advertised
As willing and deodorized,
Or aviators flying fast
As rumor through the startled vast,
Arriving, bold and handsome men,
In time to fly right back again,
Or horses eating oats galore,
Or men at peace, or peace at war,

Or puppies yipping just to yip
Because their hearts are young and flip
And sounding quite by accident
Precisely like a Great Event,
Or measles, marigolds, and mumps,
Or sitting on contented rumps.

I sat him down to honest beer
And thought of many a yesteryear,
And watched a thirst, too proud to halt,
Enschnozzle foam and gurgle malt;
"Oh, friend," said I, and "Friend," I said,
"A blessing on your balding head;
Enjoy your lager while you may—
Tomorrow is a tougher day.
The world, while you inhale your hops,
Is wobbling on its malaprops,
Is dimming out and failing fast
And falling on its mizzenmast,
Is full of bombs and soviets,
Diurnal snorts, nocturnal sweats
And frantic people in gazettes,
Of brambles, scrambles and luctations,
Brabbles, scrabbles, creeds and nations,
Babbling, braying, bruiting, chirping,
Rumbling, bumbling, mumbling, burping,
Cramps and spasms in its drain,
Fissions in its cellophane,
Boiling pundits in its fissions—
And may not last three more editions."
I fixed him with a humid eye—
"Give out, my friend, and prophesy."

He pondered ceiling, pondered wall,
And thus addressed us, one and all—

"The river snoozes through the valley;
The well still stands in Rooster's Alley;
The boys play ball in Dugan's Lane
And scatter when they hit a pane;
The way the sparrows peck the ground
You'd think that horses were around;
The kids squeeze mud between their toes
And Jake is going to marry Rose;
The plums are ripe on Chestnut Street;
The cantaloupes are special sweet;
Gelb, the glazier, talks and talks
And eats a herring as he walks;
Lilacs fell on Lizzie's hat
While standing by the fence to chat;
In Golden's garden, apple leaves
And fireflies are thick as thieves;
In spring and summer, after dark,
There's going's-on in Harvey's Park;
Free lunch is back in all the bars;
My nephew knows the names of stars;
Luke the Loafer's mother died
And for once he really cried,
Told Mrs. Pugh and Mrs. Hassel
He felt like a deserted castle;
Bauer's yard is full of pups;
The fields are nuts with buttercups;
At night the culm-banks glow like stoves
And bakers shovel out fresh loaves
And people, swatting flies in droves,
Turn their heads, expand their noses
To get the smell of bread and roses;
Dingle's boy is going to college—
He always had a thirst for knowledge;
He says he wants to build a bridge
From Laurel Hill to Warrior Ridge;

My missus makes gefüllte fish
So good you want to eat the dish,
And beef with barley on the bone
That when you eat you kind of moan . . ."
He paused, a veil upon his phiz—
"And that's about the way it is."

I brushed the barley from my brain
And thus addressed my friend again—
"My friend," said I, "I see the scene,
I know exactly what you mean.
Your algebra has mastered all:
Into each rain some life must fall,
As into beer some luckless fly;
Tomorrow, friend, it may be I—
But, till I hear my special drum,
I'm taking no viaticum;
I'm tending to my little garden
And asking no man's pence or pardon,
And sharing, as I have to share,
But not a brussels sprout to care.
The world's a weed, as well I know,
And rankles where you let it grow,
And since begat begat begat,
Is always falling on its pratt
And crushing folk beneath the drear
Expanse of its capricious rear
And getting up and reeling on
And spoiling eve and shaming dawn.
Henceforth, it's falling on its own—
We'll have some beef upon the bone."

My friend he smiled a smile so faint
It seemed to marry is to ain't;
The sun was drowsing on his head
As, "That's the way it is," he said.

[224]

From Ruth
Christmas - 1948.

mephitic

mastodonic

exacerbate
exiguous
floriverous
concatenated

priapic